COLORFUL MISSOURI

Photographs Selected by Edward King

Introduction by Bill Nunn

University of Missouri Press
Columbia, 1988

St. Louis skyline. LARRY CONAWAY

Copyright © 1988 by
The Curators of the University of Missouri
University of Missouri Press, Columbia, Missouri 65211
Printed and bound in Hong Kong
All rights reserved

∞™ This paper meets the minimum requirements of
the American National Standard for Permanence of Paper
for Printed Library Materials, Z39.48, 1984.

For CIP data, see p. 128.

COLORFUL MISSOURI

Blazing stars in Prairie State Park. DAVID ULMER

Overleaf: Barn near Hermann. DAN JOHNSON

Kansas City skyline. YVONNE ELLSWORTH

*Dedicated to the photographers
who made this book possible.*

Sunset on the Missouri River near Easley. BILL HELVEY

Publisher's Preface

This collection of photographs by photographers from throughout Missouri is a result of a general call for color photographs about the state. The idea of putting together a book like this was untried, but the response was quite encouraging. A hundred and fifty photographers submitted over a thousand photographs, and the job of selecting slightly over a hundred for the book was made difficult by having to choose between so many excellent ones. Roger Berg, current manager of Columbia Photo & Video, has been involved in numerous photography shows and told us that the response would be good, but we did not expect the great number of excellent photographs that we ultimately received.

As you will see from the biographical sketches that begin on page 124, the fifty-five photographers who are represented in this collection include both professionals who ply their craft every day and Sunday photographers who devote their leisure time to the medium. The length of experience with photography ranges from a retired executive who has pursued the hobby for several decades to a high school student who is perhaps just beginning a photographic journey that will last a lifetime. And the photographers live in many different areas of the state, from Kirksville in the north to Holts Summit in the center to Springfield in the southwest.

Two principal criteria were used in making the selection of photographs: first, quality of image and composition of subject matter were considered; second, the subject matter itself was weighed with the goal of having as much diversity as possible in the final selection, in order to show the diverse and colorful face of Missouri. Missouri is a state with many photographic opportunities—horseback riders by a spring pool, an art class under cherry blossoms in Forest Park, a bicycle race through Penn Valley Park, cattle feeding at dusk, wildlife gazing curiously into the camera, and the many landscapes and sunsets that are a memorable part of the Missouri scene. The photographers have shared with us their way of seeing the life and the countryside around us, and it is a rich celebration.

The University of Missouri Press wishes to thank each photographer who submitted work to be considered for this volume. We regret that space limitations did not allow more work to included. We also thank Roger Berg for his advice and support, which made the call and gathering of photographs run very smoothly; his active endorsement contributed greatly to the strong response and to the resulting reservoir of excellent photographs. Also helpful were James F. Keefe of Jefferson City and Ray Rothenberger of the University of Missouri–Columbia, who aided us with accurate identification of wildlife and plants.

We hope that you will enjoy the confirmation offered in the following pages of the beauty and vitality of Missouri's landscape and culture.

Colorful Missouri: Views through Old Windows

It's . . . well, incongruous. At least. But that's Missouri . . . too.

I'm writing this in our office. It's an Old World style, thirteen-room farmhouse, almost as old as Missouri itself, and its pristine primitiveness is unmarred by any modern amenity. It's early Sunday morning and quiet in the country. The fire in the Cole AirTight woodstove is murmuring peacefully, and from the outside I can hear the cheerful chattings of bluebirds feeling nature's urge to start their familial househunting in annual rites as old as the land.

Up on the hill "in town" at Loose Creek, Father Bill Flanagan will be leading his parishioners in another ritual, the centuries-old celebration of the Mass. In his soft Irish brogue, he'll say the words in English now instead of in Latin, but otherwise the ceremony is scarcely changed from the days of 150 years ago when Father Helias brought German Catholicism into this region.

This picturesque farmhouse would look at home on any *strasse* in Kaiserwerth, Germany, where the Dohmans came from in 1836. Its white stucco, fading and flaking away from old red bricks in many places, almost gleams in the morning sun. Under the roof's wide overhang, pale green shutters outline the dun-trimmed casement windows. And it's easy to imagine the "scrub *deutsch*" lady of the house polishing the huge flat limestone floors downstairs.

But through the wavy glass of the front windows, diagonally across the field below Huber's big red barn, I can see 1988 traffic streaming to and from the blinking neon sign that marks "Willibrand's Junction" where U.S. Routes 63 and 50 join for a twelve-mile run west into Jefferson City, the state capital.

And these words are being spewed out by an electronic typewriter that "interfaces" (so the salesman said) with our computer at home. It's as new as high technology can make it—until tomorrow. So this must be 1988.

This anachronistic incongruity seems apropos when trying to fashion words to depict this place called Missouri. And the location fits.

See, on the map, that tilted T junction where Route 63 from the south runs into Route 50, a loose red string tying St. Louis and Kansas City together? The Dohman-Boessen House sits at the upper edge on that blue squiggle, the Maries River. And about a lobbed rifle shot to the southeast is our roof, a steep slope of dull-silver tin glimpsed through the quick gap in the trees.

Missouri is all around us, and the view from down here in the bottom is as wide as the sky, at least in my mind's eye.

Straight out the front window, Missouri is a field of corn stalks, bent and broken last November by Gussie Boessen's efficient gleaner and battered by winter. Over the Maries and on west beyond the trees and the Osage River, there are 150 more miles of Missouri. This was the country of the Osages—and few were the tribes that cared to dispute their reign. It's painted blue now with the waters of "Mid-America's Vacation Land," the Lake of the Ozarks, and Truman Lake. And when the sun leaves Missouri this afternoon, it will fleck the skyline of Kansas City along the Kaw and the Missouri, then gild the fields of Kansas with gold.

I can see more Missouri in my imagination, another 150 miles or so of it, out the side window to the north. Past the Kliethermes ("Kleethammer," the old-timers pronounce it) corn field and over the far fringe of wooded hills, the Osage joins the Big Muddy. On its north bank, unmarked Cote Sans Dessein ("Hill without Design"), once in the running as a site for the state capital, denotes the French flavor of early settlements. Its river site also marks generally the southern edge of the state's Northern Plains, the great sweep of level to gently rolling land scoured by the long-ago glacier as it pulled back all the way to Ioway. Look left, to the west, and there's St. Joseph and the Pony Express and Missouri River country. Toward the east is

Sunrise on Binder Lake, Jefferson City. JULIE SMITH

Hannibal and the Mississippi. And in between are the Grand and Chariton rivers, with the Clarence Cannon Dam and Mark Twain Lake on the Salt recent man-made additions.

From the second-story back windows, to the east, Missouri stretches for another 100 or so crow miles—up the sloping pasture to the first ridge of cedars, then ridge over ridge into the Gasconade region, the Bourbeuse and the Meramec river-breaks, and on to St. Louis, the aptly named Gateway to the West. And the in-between is typically incongruous Missouri—the underground wonders of Onondaga and Meramec caverns and the above-ground dazzle and thrills of Six Flags Over Mid-America at Eureka.

The view from the fourth-floor attic window looks toward more than 200 miles of Missouri—from south toward Westphalia, the "capital" of this midstate German enclave; through the Big Piney region around Fort Leonard Wood, the Army's giant Engineer Corps base; and into the steep hills and valleys of the Current River–Big Spring country of the south-central Ozarks, where big timber once grew before the loggers came.

This south-central area is all anchored east and west by another Missouri dichotomy—on the west by the scenery-and-pleasure-business Shepherd of the Hills country, where early settlers lived lean and frugally on hardscrabble land, and on the east by the black-rich Mississippi delta, where cotton planters fashioned a Bootheel replica of the Deep South.

＊　　＊　　＊

As Americans we have been reared on a rich heritage of tomorrows—of always greener pastures "over there," of anticipation of events to come or to make happen, of places to see and to conquer around the next bend in the river or over the next hill. In Missouri nature nurtured that heritage into full flower by strewing a grab bag of growing things over a geological potpourri beset and blessed by a capricious climate. All of which produces year-round crops of "Well, would you look here . . . !"

Each of us looks through different windows—or sees different views from the same windows. Here are a few I've enjoyed opening.

＊　　＊　　＊

The conductor sang out his last "Alll-aa-booaarrd," clanged the steel door shut, and the Missouri Pacific *Colorado Eagle* shuddered and squeaked, then eased out of Kansas City's Union Station bound east. City lights winked through the coach windows from the dusk of a late November evening. Then warehouses and multi-colored street lights slipped by in blurs; then, faster, the iron wheels and the creaks and bumps rolled into a lulling rhythm as the *Eagle* left the city and snaked its way through the darkening night of the countryside.

Away from the river hills of the city, the land would look like Kansas out there for a while, flat and open. Lights from the scattered farm homes grew from pinpoints on the dark canvas of land and sky into beams from kitchen windows, then faded back into the night.

Pleasant Hill was the first stop. The little depot glowed warmly from the cold as doors banged and friendly voices bantered over mail sacks and boxes. Then, quickly, the doors slammed shut again and the train eased on into the darkness.

Warrensburg would be next, home of the Mules, the athletic name for the "teachers' college" that became Central Missouri State University. Then came Sedalia, once a MoPac division point and "Queen City of the Prairie." Over on Main Street—on the "sporting strip," as local residents decorously called the bawdiest red light district east of Denver—Scott Joplin had made musical history with his ragtime piano at the Maple Leaf Club. And after 1899, when local music publisher John Stark published Joplin's composition named after the club, the whole nation went "ragged music" crazy.

California was a Moniteau County example of Missourians' penchant for exotic and "other places" names. (A story passed along by Robert L. Ramsay, though, says the town's christening was due to another penchant common among early Missourians: supposedly California Wilson offered to treat workers raising the logs for the town's first saloon to two gallons of whiskey if they would name the settlement after him, and the impromptu referendum understandably passed unanimously.) Then the tracks lay along the Missouri River, past Sandy Hook and Marion, the other site bypassed in the contest for the state capital. We were deep now into mid-Missouri and rolling toward the capital, Jefferson City.

Along the bluffs west of town, the train whistled its coming. Suddenly, through a break in the sliced-off bluffs, the lighted dome of the majestic Capitol—built of Carthage limestone quarried near "down home"—filled the windows. The train slowed and stopped.

A half-dozen passengers stepped down and disappeared into the red brick station, then through the front doors into waiting family cars or the two or three Yellow Cabs lined up on the brick street.

My cracked and peeling Gladstone bag wasn't heavily loaded, and I headed up the steep Monroe Street hill for "town," a couple of blocks away. The hotel—the Central, not the Governor or the Missouri—would be up that way. And the newspaper office, too, where tomorrow I hoped to pass muster

with a gruff-sounding editor named Chet Krause and be on my way to making journalistic history.

Halfway up the hill, I stopped. The Capitol lit up the end of Capitol Avenue. And lights were on in the next block at the newspaper office; the night staff would be working on the morning paper. This was a two-paper-a-day town—with a Capitol and government and politics, three hotels, and solid old brick houses on river country hills.

Beyond the station, out there in the night, the river was rolling muddily down to the Mississippi, much as it had in 1804 when Lewis and Clark poled and keelboated past here. But it surely was tamer now than it had been in the late 1800s when steamboats guided by devil-take-the-hindmost pilots delivered people and "goods" all the way to the headwaters in the Big Sky country. And it was more civilized now than in the mid-1800s when boatloads of German immigrants landed here and at nearby points to settle and to put their imprint on this land which reminded them of their native Rhineland and Bavaria . . .

The river and the hills swallowed the sounds and the voices at the station, and I watched the *Eagle,* long rows of rectangular yellow streaks, slip past the bluffs and head on downriver to St. Louis.

It was the first time I had felt a sense of place. Here, I thought, I had to live.

*   *   *

My new "beat" would be Missouri, I was told by my new boss at the Department of Conservation. In that department, that meant *outdoor* Missouri. Growing up at Granby, I had spent a lot of time outdoors—but delivering the morning *Joplin Globe* and afternoon *News-Herald,* not hunting and fishing. In the broomsedge and brush around the "tailin' piles" and shaft dumps left from the lead mining days, I *had* trapped a few rabbits. I'd even shot a few of them and some squirrels with my single-shot .22 rifle and stunned a few more with a slingshot. But now I would need to learn about nature and her "critters"—and how man needed to live with them so he wouldn't be the loser by winning the ages-old struggle of the survival of the fittest.

The department was only fifteen years old then. In 1937 Missourians, fed up with the old political Fish and Game Department, had uncharacteristically become innovators. They voted to establish the Conservation Commission as a virtually autonomous constitutional agency; its job was to "do something" about the sad state of wildlife affairs. And they included forests, too.

The boss was Dan Saults, former editor of the weekly *Knob Noster Item*. An incurably romantic word-wielder, he set the linguistic tone for explaining scientific findings and decisions in understandable English, clothed with lofty purpose. My immediate tutor would be Don Wooldridge, the chief photographer. Our assignment was to put pictures and words with the conservation message—to the tune Saults hummed.

*   *   *

It was a moonless night and the sky reflected muddled shadows on Noblett Lake, a small patch of water in the woods of Mark Twain Forest near Willow Springs. We'd spent the day as Wooldridge, snorkeling in dimestore gear, tried to photograph largemouth bass in the shallows. Now we were trying to entice them into supplying the next morning's breakfast.

Oaks and hickories and a few pines rimmed the little lake, and a soft wind basted their shadows into a wavering skirt. They were second-growth trees, mostly, replacements from the intensive logging at the turn of the century that had cleared off most of the virgin timber in these Ozark hills.

Don and I savored the silence of friends, noting an occasional owl hooting softly from the dark or shrugging at the splash of a lunker (of course) breaking water—always out of casting range. With muffled strokes, Don had worked us into a little inlet and we lay still in the watery shadows.

I watched the dark ripples of a Hula Popper as, cast after cast, I jerked it, rested it, jerked it along the shore. Suddenly, alongside the canoe a loud SLAP startled me and rocked the canoe. Don insisted that *I* had rocked it, that the prowling beaver wasn't *that big*. They did that with their wide, flat tails, he told me from his store of superior knowledge, to warn fellow beavers that we had encroached upon their territory.

Whatever its purpose, it ended our fishing for the night. In my sleeping bag that night I imagined I could hear, wafting up from the dying campfire, the ghostly laughter of Jed Smith and John Colter and all the other tough mountain men from Missouri who had opened the West by trapping those critters.

With improved habitat, the beaver had taken care of his own "comeback." And with its carefully researched and planned programs, the Conservation Department had started turning a decimated wildlife population back into a renewable natural resource.

Still fired with the dedication of pioneering, department employees were turning history around. "Little Dixie" Robb, with his big pipe and southern drawl, led the deer program, which in fifty quick years would swell a meager herd of 3,000 animals into one with an annual hunters' kill of more than 100,000. Kenny Sadler was conniving ways of dealing with the wary turkey that would repeat that success—with both spring and fall seasons becoming annual events for a bird that had been at one time hunted to near extinction.

Jack Stanford was learning more about quail than almost any biologist in the country. And Charlie and Libby Schwartz, with his incredibly accurate and artistic black-and-white renderings and her thorough documentation and words, were showing and telling the public the whole conservation story.

The list was long. And these and many other people were not only opening new windows in Missouri; they were changing forever the views to be seen for generations to come.

*   *   *

It was 1960 and the growl of the bulldozer was heard across the land.

The highway builders were remaking the map of Missouri. They were doubling—and more—the width of those red lines of major highways crisscrossing the state. They were running them straight through big cities and around small towns, across big rivers and through mountains.

They were building the Interstate Highway System. It was the nation's largest peacetime construction project—and Missouri again had led the way. On 2 August 1956 it became the first state in the nation to let contracts for work on the ambitious program, and a few weeks later it became the first to start construction.

There were three history-making contracts: one for a stretch of I-44 in Laclede County and two on I-70, one in the City of St. Louis and one in St. Charles County. The first construction started on the St. Charles project.

The plans for the mammoth undertaking called for building 41,000 miles of divided, four-lane highways. Missouri's share would be 1,147 miles. And the figures involved boggled the mind:

Enough dirt to bury Connecticut—knee deep.

Enough concrete for 80 Hoover Dams; enough tar and asphalt for 35 million driveways; enough steel for 170 Empire State Buildings; enough culvert and drain pipe for the water and sewage systems of six cities as big as Chicago . . .

It was a project of "biggests" and "firsts"—and it became the last time that highway engineers would wear unsmudged White Hats.

As Missouri entered its second century of statehood, the need for good highways was as obvious as a pothole. Eager to "Get Missouri Out of the Mud," as the slogan for the 1927 bond issue of $75 million said, voters generally gave the engineers carte blanche—"do what you gotta do" to get the job done.

They did the job well. By 1960 they had built 32,000 miles of state highways, the nation's seventh largest system, and the department was recognized as one of the nation's best. The highway engineers let their work speak for itself, and generally it was an effective spokesman—until the blank checks of the Interstate system started getting bigger.

The size and the complexities before the pouring of concrete needed some explaining. "Bypass," for instance, became an ugly word, defined in places like Boonville on "old" U.S. 40 as a siphoning off of the lifeblood of traffic, leaving the town to wither away. At one point, so the probably apocryphal story goes, Chief Engineer Rex Whitton "couldn't buy a cup of coffee" in the Cooper County seat. Even the farmers, like Milton Sieckman, "fought its coming through here tooth and toenail." But five years later, he "couldn't be happier."

The new highway sliced through 27 acres of his land, much of it rich, black bottomland. "All of us around here figured the new highway wouldn't help us much," he said. "We thought we'd still use the old highway (Missouri Route 98) into Boon-

ville. But about all you'll find on 98 now are trucks and corn pickers.

"Times have changed. We need highways like this. I just don't see how that much traffic ever got through downtown Boonville."

Moving mountains was relatively easy. But people and industries in big cities could change lives . . .

Carl Sciuto's Stile-Craft precision-product plant on the Hill in south St. Louis sat in the way of the new I-44. It was a landmark on the Italian Hill but it had to go.

When the highway engineers and right-of-way people came to his office, he jotted down a figure on a piece of paper and laid it face down on his desk.

It was within $37,000 of the department offer, which he accepted. "We needed more space anyway," he said. And he built a new building with 87,000 square feet, 33,000 more than he'd had.

Others couldn't move. The new I-70 in Montgomery County—replacing old 40's infamous Mineola Hill—needed 43 acres of Graham family land. It was the third time highways had cut through it—first the Old Trails Road, then U.S. 40, and now I-70. And with the new highway's limited access, Frances Darnell's one-mile trip to her daughter's home would be multiplied by fourteen.

But this fourth generation of Grahams to live in the old farmhouse was philosophical. She laughed as she told about the plight of some Wellsville friends who visited her.

"They said they knew the way," she said. "And they finally did make it—after they went all the way over to Williamsburg and back."

The building of the Interstate system, like no other projects before it, strained the traditional ties of a man to his property, a basic heritage in a country built by people living off the land. But its building, needed to better serve a new era, made its planners and builders more conscious of working with people.

It was a story that needed telling—a story of people whose everyday work, building new windows and new views of Missouri, added up to history.

*   *   *

I had stayed the night at a motel in Monett, eleven miles south of I-44, and was heading early for a visit "back home" at Granby. The morning sun would be good for taking photographs for a story we were doing on the beauty of roadside flowers.

The Interstate was fine for making time, but this morning I wanted to savor it. I drove south on Missouri 37 to Barry County Route B—supplementary roads, the department called them—and headed west.

Somewhere east of Pioneer, the blacktop road was lined on both sides with daisies, warm gold in the slanting new sun. Not a car was in sight, and yellow-breasted meadowlarks sprinkled the air with their clear notes.

I was belly down in the flowers with a close-up lens when I heard the *putter-putter* of a tractor. It was too late to pretend . . . anything. I cocked one eye off the viewfinder as the farmer drove by.

"Man," he said, almost to himself, "I sure wish I had a job like that."

I wished he did, too. But not mine.

Bill Nunn
Loose Creek, Missouri

Overleaf: Sunrise in an Ozark County pasture. BILL HARTMAN

Balloon gondola at dusk. RICKARD WALK

15

Barn near Queen City. CURTIS N. VANWYE

A hillside view at Easley. GREGORY WOLFF

18

Fishing at sunrise on a small lake north of Columbia. TONY WEIL

Fall colors on Hinkson Creek, Columbia. ROGER BERG

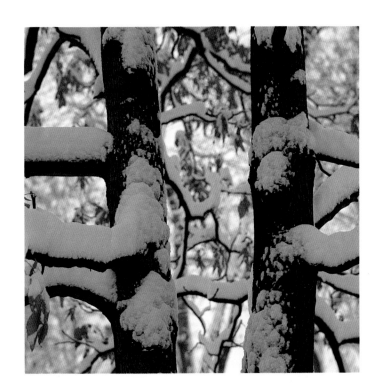

Winter in the Mark
Twain National Forest.
OLIVER SCHUCHARD

Ice on a creek in Moniteau County. LLOYD GROTJAN

After a snowstorm in Lawrence
County. THOMAS TROGDON

Overleaf: The Missouri River bluffs
near Bluffton. MARK PELTON

Prairie grass at Cuivre River State Park. PETER J. GLASS

Flowers on a catalpa tree. MARK PELTON

Rue anemone. CHARLES F. MORGAN

The south steps of the State
Capitol. BRUCE MATHEWS

The Harry S. Truman
home, Independence.
E. CAROL CREASON-WESTON

Fog shrouds the dome of the State Capitol, Jefferson City. HELEN L. CALLENTINE

Bright sunlight highlights the contemporary architecture of the Medical Sciences Building at the
University of Missouri–Columbia. GREGORY WOLFF

The University of Missouri–Columbia campus. BART LARSON

Mark Twain home, Hannibal. OLIVER SCHUCHARD

Ballooning on the St. Louis riverfront. PETER J. GLASS

Outboards racing at George Winter Park, Fenton. RICKARD WALK

Hot rod show at Lindenwood College in St. Charles. ROGER J. MCCARTHY

The Snake Saturday parade in North Kansas City. RUSS MEHL

A three year old at Silver Dollar City. ROGER J. MCCARTHY

Opposite: Riverboat at Worlds of Fun. BRUCE MATHEWS

37

Firemen provide a treat for St. Louis children during the Veiled Prophet celebration. GARY T. MCGUIRE

A pep rally readies the Redbirds for the World Series. LEWIS A. PORTNOY

Overleaf: Busch Stadium, St. Louis. LEWIS A. PORTNOY

Racing in Penn Valley Park,
Kansas City. MARGARITE HOEFLER

The *Mark Twain* cruises the Mississippi below Hannibal. CHARLES T. ERWIN

Antique shop in Arrow Rock. DAVID J. WALKER

Restaurant interior at Laclede's Landing on the St. Louis riverfront. DAVID GOLD

A contemporary Missouri-made basket with several antiques. DAVID GOLD

Spinning wool into yarn at the Sheep Festival in Bethel. ALBERT J. COPLEY

Cornhusk dolls at Missouri Town 1855, Blue Springs. GREG SLEE

Riverboat on the Missouri River at Jefferson City at sunrise. JULIE SMITH

Great blue heron
at Fellows Lake,
near Springfield.
MARTA HAMMOND

Hunters' Cave in Three Creeks State Forest, south of Columbia. DAVID J. WALKER

Waterfall in Hickory Canyon, Ste. Genevieve County. GARRETT ROBERTS

Old turbine and housing at Boze Mill Spring on the Eleven Point River. MARK PELTON

A whitetail fawn in Gasconade County. CHRISTINE STRUTTMAN

Killdeer on the banks of the Mississippi. BRIAN K. LOCKWOOD

A young great horned owl in the Mark Twain National Forest. DOUG K. HARDESTY

Screech owl at the Tyson Research Center, St. Louis County. BRIAN K. LOCKWOOD

Monarch butterfly. BRIAN K. LOCKWOOD

Bobcat. BRIAN K. LOCKWOOD

Overleaf: Typical evening sky near Springfield. LEAH DRENNON

Wild turkeys in the Tyson Research Center, St. Louis County. BLAINE A. ULMER

Geese on partially ice-covered lake in Swope Park, Kansas City. MARK A. STYLES

Overleaf: Blue and snow geese at Squaw Creek National Wildlife Refuge. MARGARITE HOEFLER

Eastern bluebird. BRIAN K. LOCKWOOD

A reconstructed mill built near the site of the old Brawley family mill, near Centerville. DR. RUSSELL M. KEELING

Flyfishing at Maramec Spring. GARRY ROSE

Round Spring runoff. NANCY L. THOMPSON

Canoeing on the Meramec River. LLOYD GROTJAN

Kayaking in St. Francis River rapids near Fredericktown. DAVID ULMER

Elephant Rocks State Park. OLIVER SCHUCHARD

On horseback at Alley Spring. EARL A. JETT

Swimmers at Johnson's Shut-Ins State Park. DR. RUSSELL M. KEELING

The sun sets behind the ruins at Ha Ha Tonka State Park. ROBERT COLVIN

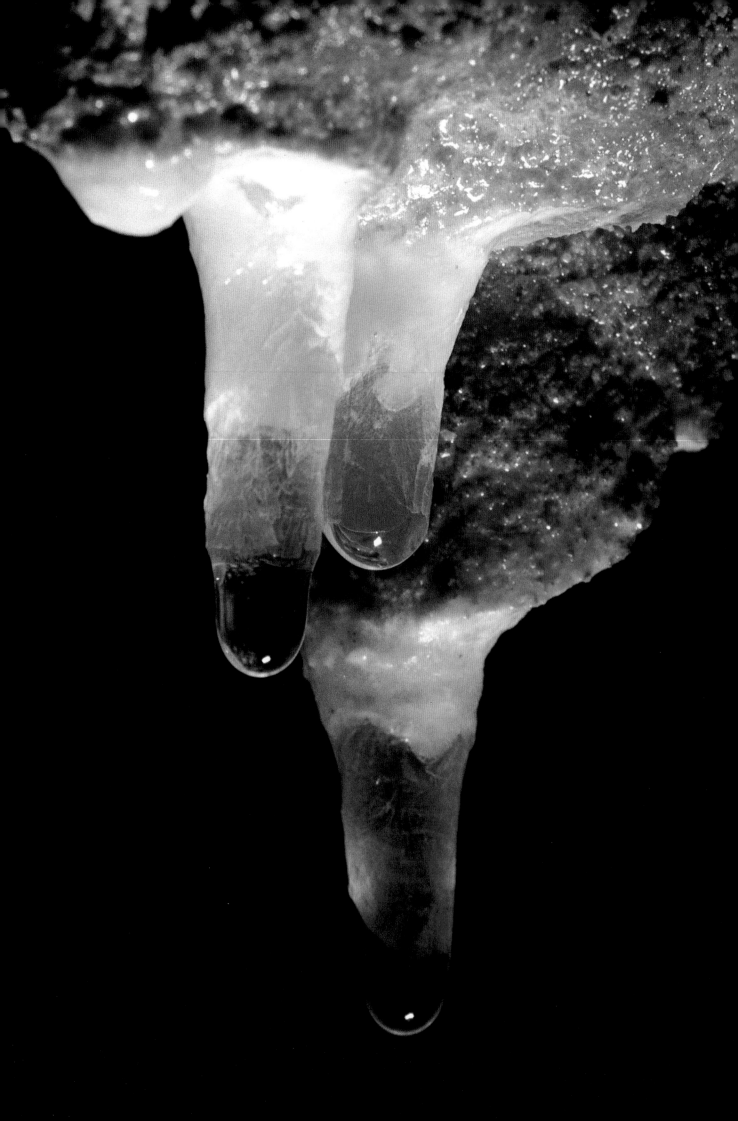

Little Hamilton Cave, Meramec State Park. RICKARD WALK

Stalactites with soda straws in Fisher Cave, Meramec State Park. RICKARD WALK

Mill at Alley Spring. OLIVER SCHUCHARD

Dogwoods and wild blue phlox in Osage County. OLIVER SCHUCHARD

78

Stream bank in the Big Piney Wilderness Area. OLIVER SCHUCHARD

Logger's Lake, near Bunker. GARRY ROSE

Overleaf: Bald cypress in the Mingo National Wildlife Refuge. DAVID ULMER

81

Sandy Creek Covered Bridge in Jefferson County. PETER J. GLASS

Ice coats a meadow at Three Creeks State Forest, south of Columbia. MARK PELTON

Sheep, cattle, and a well-stocked woodlot on a Boone County farm. GAY BUMGARNER

Picking pumpkins near Sibley, Jackson County. GREG SLEE

Storefront in Ponce De Leon, Stone County. MARTA HAMMOND

Lightning in Lawrence County. THOMAS TROGDON

Feeding ground corn on a Boone County farm. TONY WEIL

Newborn calf in Christian County. MARTA HAMMOND

The Pete Kremer farm in Buck Holler, Osage County. GARY R. KREMER

Grain storage bins in Scotland County. ALBERT J. COPLEY

Sunset on a Lawrence County farm. BILL HELVEY

View through window of abandoned farmhouse near Hermann. THOMAS TROGDON

Overleaf: Freshly mown hay in Boone County. GAY BUMGARNER

Sunset after a storm, north of Jefferson City. VALENTINE H. GERMANN

Ox-eye daisies fill a field near Westboro. HARLAN SMITH

St. Marcus Evangelical Church at Rhineland. CHARLES F. MORGAN

Overleaf: A rustic wall in Cape Girardeau. DAVID GOLD

Wagon wheel. DAVID GOLD

A barbwire collection at The Livery in Fair Grove. MARTA HAMMOND

Quilts displayed at Frankclay in St. Francois County. ELIZABETH M. CROSBY

Overleaf: Bridges over the Mississippi at St. Louis. JIM SOKOLIK

Lyceum Theatre, Arrow Rock. BRUCE MATHEWS

Lexington home in Queen Anne style. SHELLEY L. DENNIS

Dome of the Cathedral of the Immaculate Conception, Kansas City. BRUCE MATHEWS

Overleaf: Barge traffic on the Mississippi River near Winfield. CHARLES F. MORGAN

Art class in Forest Park. LEWIS A. PORTNOY

Fishing in St. Louis's Forest Park. JIM SOKOLIK

Kansas City Zoo. BRUCE MATHEWS

Detail of fountain by Carl Milles at Union Station, St. Louis. DAVID GOLD

Giralda Tower on the Country Club Plaza in Kansas City. VALENTINE GERMANN

Chinese Pavilion in Tower Grove
Park, St. Louis. QUINTA SCOTT

116

Victoria water lilies at the Missouri Botanical Garden in St. Louis. LLOYD GROTJAN

Flowers behind a fence in St. Louis's Central West End. DAVID GOLD

Boston ivy and bindweed flower. LLOYD GROTJAN   119

Plaza Square Apartments with Union Station tower in background, St. Louis. DAVID GOLD

St. Louis riverfront. CHARLES WEISHAUPT

The State Ballet of Missouri, based in the Lyric Theatre in Kansas City. BRUCE MATHEWS

A sculpture in the Oriental collection of the Nelson-Atkins Museum of Art, Kansas City. BRUCE MATHEWS

Greer Spring, Oregon County. DICK KAHOE

Contributing Photographers

Roger Berg (p. 20), manager of Columbia Photo & Video, has been an avid photographer for thirty years and has been active in Missouri amateur and professional photography and the photo industry for twenty years, but still spends his leisure time taking color slides of nature, underwater, and travel subjects, as well as experimenting with new products and techniques. He makes Cibachrome color enlargements from his own slides as well as commercially in Columbia Photo's lab—a hobby within a career.

Gay Bumgarner (pp. 86, 96–97) was a professional landscape designer in Columbia, Missouri, until her interest in nature and wildlife led her to change to photography as a career. Her work has been published in *Audubon* field guides, in *Birders World,* in calendars for *Audubon, Sierra Club,* and *Landmark,* and in other places. She sells her own line of Missouri photography notecards.

Helen L. Callentine (p. 28) became involved in photography, using color slide and black-and-white film, while traveling in the Army Nurse Corps. She learned black-and-white film and print processing when assigned in a remote area. After retiring as a hospital nursing consultant, she has become even more enthusiastic in color slide and negative processing and printing. She is a member of the Jefferson City Photo Club.

Robert Colvin (p. 75) is a lifelong resident of Cole County, Missouri, and as a sales representative he travels extensively throughout the central Missouri region. For over a decade he has carried his camera wherever he goes, photographing scenic areas, historic sites, and wildlife. Although he has traveled throughout the United States, he never grows tired of photographing the beauty of Missouri. He has won numerous prizes and awards for his photographs and is always ready to share his enthusiasm and skills with others.

Larry Conaway (p. 4) first became interested in photography through his work as an electronic engineer for McDonnell Douglas. His photographs have been published on billboards, postcards, brochures, posters, calendars, book covers, and magazines, and one was used on the cover of *Decision,* a national magazine produced by the Billy Graham Evangelistic Association. He is anxiously awaiting his retirement so he can pursue this interest full-time.

Albert J. Copley (pp. 47, 92) is associate professor of geology at Northeast Missouri State University. He uses photography for geological illustration in his teaching, but his interest in photography has expanded into fields other than geology, and he has had numerous pictures published in a variety of textbooks and magazines. He loves to travel, which provides him with an endless opportunity to use his skills in photography.

E. Carol Creason-Weston (p. 29) became interested in photography as a child when her parents gave her a Kodak camera as a gift. She graduated to several Canon 35mm cameras with which she has won three awards in local and state contests since 1984. Carol enjoys capturing moments of her beloved Ozark hills, their people, and the many places she and her husband travel to. This hobby serves as a creative, relaxing world away from her counseling career.

Elizabeth (Betty) Crosby (p. 105) has been an enthusiastic photographer since the age of twelve, nearly sixty years. Extensive travels to many remote areas of the world have provided much of her subject matter. Many of her photographs have won awards in international competitions. Since 1981, between foreign trips, Crosby has concentrated on photographing the state of Missouri, and she has prepared two photo books in black and white documenting Missouri's 114 counties. Now, with her husband, she is continuing that documentation in color.

Shelley L. Dennis (p. 108) gives credit for her early interest in photography to an eighth-grade English teacher who shared that hobby with her students. Now a high school science teacher, Shelley has combined her love of nature and travel with her love for the camera by focusing her freelance career on landscapes and wild flowers. Victorian architecture has also been a favorite pastime of hers, and when she is not teaching, Shelley can be found on weekend trips around the state, documenting the landscapes and buildings of her native Missouri.

Leah Drennon (pp. 60–61), a student at Kickapoo High School in Springfield, has attended photography classes at the Springfield Art Museum. She enjoys traveling throughout Missouri photographing various subjects. The sky is one subject that fascinates her with its ever-changing cloud formations. Leah hopes one day to make photography her career.

Yvonne Ellsworth (p. 5) is from Chicago and has lived in the Kansas City area for sixteen years. A professional photographer for eight years, she enjoys using 4 x 5 equipment and printing her own black-and-white work. She specializes in architecture and landscapes and has won competitions at the Kansas City Arts Commission and Kaw Valley, Kansas. She also works in the Education Department at the Nelson-Atkins Museum of Art and free-lances for *KC Life Downtown*.

Charles T. Erwin (p. 44) has enjoyed photography as a hobby for twenty-five years. His subjects have ranged from the usual family birthdays and vacations to flora and fauna. Recently, he has joined the McDonnell Douglas Corporation Photo Club and has become interested in photography as an art form. Black-and-white photography and working in his darkroom are part of his newly expanded interests.

Valentine Germann (pp. 98–99, 115) has been an avid photographer since he edited the Carrollton High School *Tales of Troy*. His special photographic interest at present is the interaction of earth, sky, and cloud in his home state. He currently combines vocation with avocation by working in retail camera sales in Columbia.

Peter J. Glass (pp. 26, 33, 84), a University of Missouri–St. Louis graduate and a resident of Florissant, photographs nature, landscapes, and a variety of subjects around St. Louis and throughout the state. He works both in color and in black and white. He credits his affiliation with the St. Louis Camera Club as a source of learning and motivation. His current ambition is to pursue professional editorial and commercial work.

David Gold (pp. 46, 102–3, 104, 114, 119, 120), a graduate of the University of Missouri–Columbia with a graphics major, taught fashion drawing at Stephens College in Columbia, Missouri. He trained under one of the nation's top advertising photographers and established his own studio in 1982 as Gold, Inc., specializing in 8 x 10 format. Winner of Flair and New York Ad Club awards, Gold also represents other advertising suppliers. He has worked on many national accounts such as Ralston Purina, McDonald's, and Anheuser-Busch.

Lloyd Grotjan (pp. 23, 70, 118, 119) has been involved in photography from an early age. Grotjan owns Full Spectrum Photo, a commercial photography firm in Jefferson City. His work has been published in numerous magazines and periodicals and is on permanent display throughout the state.

Marta Hammond (pp. 50–51, 88, 91, 104) became her high school yearbook photographer sixteen years ago because her father had the only camera available. The experience initiated a love for photography that has become a special part of her life as park ranger and zookeeper (she is a naturalist by education) and now as owner of SkyLight Photography. She and her husband take great pleasure in being outdoors and enjoying the beauty of creation, whether they are traveling on foot, on horseback, or by plane.

Doug Hardesty (p. 57) is currently finishing his bachelor's degree in Fisheries and Wildlife at the University of Missouri–Columbia. Doug has been taking pictures for eight years. His subjects are primarily landscapes and wildlife. His photographs have appeared in *Missouri Conservationist* and the MFA Calendar.

Bill Hartman (pp. 16–17) has had a keen interest in photography since the age of fourteen. While he has pursued a full-time career in a nonphotographic job, his hobby has led to his photographs being published in a number of local and national magazines and newspapers. He has been staff photographer for *The Ozarks Mountaineer* for the last five years. He is also a volunteer photographer for the Raptor Rehabilitation and Propagation Project.

Bill Helvey (pp. 6, 94) has an enthusiasm for Missouriana, landscapes, and the rural way of life. He uses his photography as an artistic medium and has had more than fifty art and photography exhibits. His photographs have been published in *Popular Photography, Camera 35,* and *Missouri Life*. His work is regularly published by the University Extension at Lincoln University, where he is a state communications specialist.

Margarite Hoefler (pp. 42–43, 64–65) believes that her occupation as photographic printer for Architectural Fotografics in Kansas City gives her a discerning eye for color that enhances her photography of scenics and abstract nature patterns. She particularly enjoys taking photographs while on backpacking and bicycle touring trips through Missouri and around the country. She has won many awards in photo competitions and area art shows. Her work has appeared in national publications such as *Outside, Bicycling,* and *Backpacker* and in the 1988 Audubon Desk Calendar.

Earl A. Jett (p. 73) became interested in photography in 1967 as a result of viewing through a Contax 35mm SLR camera with 100mm lens attached. He is an active member of the Southwest Missouri Camera Club and the Photographic Society of America. His darkroom works usually are black-and-white toned prints from medium format (2 ¼ x 2 ¼ Hasselblad camera). His photographs have appeared in textbooks and several national magazines.

Dan Johnson (p. 2) is an active member of the St. Louis Camera Club. He takes his photography seriously but also takes pleasure in presenting humorous subjects. His photo sequence "Humor in Photography" has been shown at clubs as an incentive to include humor. Another program he developed involves photographing two or more items that represent a word or expression. For example, a salt shaker plus a flashlight battery equals the expression "assault and battery." Most of his work is done outdoors and focuses on simple details.

Dick Kahoe (p. 123) closed his studio in southwest Missouri in 1986 to return to school after a fifteen-year intermission. He is presently working on a degree or two at Central Missouri State University at Warrensburg and plans to teach at the university level. He uses a number of specialized wide-angle and panoramic cameras to photograph the beauty of Missouri's scenes.

Dr. Russell M. Keeling (pp. 67, 74), professor of communication and assistant to the president at Southwest Missouri State University, uses photography to express, among other things, his lifelong love of the Ozarks. Many of his photographs have found their way into multi-image productions he has produced or assisted with. He has also taught courses in photography and in multi-image production.

Gary Kremer (p. 93) developed an interest in landscapes and farm scenes in his rural Osage County youth. Since 1978, that interest has been nurtured by his involvement with cultural resource surveys for the Missouri Department of Natural Resources. Along with being a widely published author, Kremer has had photographs appear in *Missouri Life, Gateway Heritage,* and *American Studies.* A professor of history for sixteen years, Kremer currently serves as Missouri State Archivist.

Bart Larson (p. 30), photographer and producer of the *Missouri Calendar,* lives in Columbia, Missouri, with his wife and two daughters. Besides being a photographer, he is a free-lance writer, commercial artist, and promoter of art shows. He says that few things give him greater joy than taking outdoor photographs, particularly in the spring and fall. In the movie *Chariots of Fire,* Eric Liddell said, "God made me fast. I feel His pleasure when I run." Bart says he experiences that same pleasure when he is behind his camera attempting to capture the beauty and artistry of creation.

Brian Lockwood (pp. 55, 56, 58, 59, 66), a student at the School of Forestry, Fisheries, and Wildlife at the University of Missouri–Columbia, started photographing wildlife at the age of fifteen. His summers have been spent working for the Missouri Department of Conservation. He has worked primarily with color film, but is beginning to experiment with black and white. His photographs have appeared in *Missouri Conservationist* and newspapers across the state.

Roger J. McCarthy (pp. 35, 37) is a data processing project manager for McDonnell Douglas Corporation in St. Louis. He has been active in photography as a hobby for the past ten years. Roger enjoys all types of photography but specializes in photographing nature scenes, landscapes, and cityscapes. His subjects of interest include his family, hot rods, old cemeteries, and reflections. His work is exhibited in the Executive Center of the McDonnell Douglas Corporation in St. Louis.

Gary T. McGuire (p. 38) is a native St. Louisan and a toolmaker by trade. In love with the visual arts from a very early age, he still pursues them in such mediums as leathercraft, pen and ink, model building, painting, sketching, and photography. His affair with photography began at age eleven when, for three dollars, he purchased his first camera. He later studied photography at Florissant Valley College.

Bruce Mathews (pp. 29, 36, 108, 109, 114, 122) is a professional photographer from Kansas City specializing in location assignment work and in the production of multi-image audiovisual presentations. He is a member of the American Society of Magazine Photographers. Assignments have taken him from coast to coast, and his work has appeared in many books and magazines including *Audubon, Cosmopolitan, Golf Course Management, Club Management,* and *Guest Informant.*

Russ Mehl (p. 37) is the manager of petroleum supply and distribution for Kansas City–based Farmland Industries. He became interested in photography while serving in the Air Force in England some twenty years ago. He has won many photography contests in the Kansas City area, including the Kansas City Renaissance Festival contest. His credits include a cover for *Unity* magazine, and his work has been displayed in various malls and stores.

Charles F. Morgan (pp. 27, 101, 110–11) has been an active amateur photographer for the last ten years, spending all his available free time pursuing his love of nature and color photography. He has been an active member of the St. Louis Camera Club since 1982 and is a multi-star nature exhibitor in the Photographic Society of America. He has had a career in the engineering profession for the past thirty-three years and is currently a drafting designer with a St. Louis engineering firm.

Mark Pelton (pp. 24–25, 27, 54, 85), a forester with the Missouri Department of Conservation, enjoys photographing the natural beauty of our state. He likes to capture flowers, fall foliage, streams, and landscapes on high-quality slide film. He lives in centrally located Columbia, which gives him an opportunity to view the variety of our state's natural scenes.

Lewis A. Portnoy (pp. 39, 40–41, 113) is a photographer whose work from over two thousand assignments in sports journalism and location photography for advertising and industry has gained international respect. Since his beginning as photographer for the St. Louis Blues, Lewis has photographed nearly every major sporting event in North America. A St. Louis–based free-lance photographer, he has worked for the three television networks, major corporations, advertising agencies, and major publications, and has been active conducting photographic classes and workshops.

Garrett Roberts (p. 53), a free-lance photographer from St. Louis, enjoys exploring the natural wonders of the Missouri Ozarks, striving to create images that reveal the mysterious, spiritual aspects of nature. His award-winning photographs have appeared in juried photography exhibits and art fairs in the St. Louis area.

Garry Rose (pp. 69, 80), a native of St. Louis County, is an optical engineer for McDonnell Douglas Corporation. He enjoys combining his hobbies of camping and backpacking with his love of nature photography. He is particularly interested in macro photography and has a large collection of photographs of the flora and fauna of the woods of Missouri. Garry has sold his work to individuals, and his photos have won numerous photo contests around the St. Louis area.

Oliver Schuchard (pp. 23, 32, 72, 78, 79, 81), associate professor of photography at the University of Missouri–Columbia, has photographed the natural scene for nearly twenty years, specializing in the Missouri landscape. In addition to over one hundred exhibitions, his work is included in numerous private, institutional, and corporate collections. Two collections of his photographs of Missouri have been published, *Two Ozark Rivers* (1984) and *Missouri* (1982).

Quinta Scott (pp. 116–17) has exhibited her photographs in St. Louis and regionally. Her income is primarily from portraiture. Her photographic studies of vernacular architecture and her recent show of landscapes have received excellent reviews. Her photographs have been published in two books, *The Eads Bridge* (1979) and *Route 66* (to be published in fall 1988).

Greg Slee (pp. 48, 87), creative designer for Tension Envelope Corporation, has won numerous graphic design awards both locally and internationally. His interest in photography began as a hobby, recording his travels and gathering source material for paintings and illustrations. Now his photographs have also received recognition on their own. Both his painting and photography have been honored with blue ribbons at the Missouri State Fair. He has a special interest in the bluffs, farmland, people, and history along the Missouri River Valley.

Harlan Smith (p. 100) began photography as a hobby about four years ago. He is a member of the Kansas City Color Slide Club and has won several prizes in its annual contests. Wildlife photography is his greatest interest. He has made two trips to Africa, where he was fortunate to pursue this interest. Harlan has also been a finalist in the National Wildlife Federation yearly photo contest.

Julie Smith (pp. 8, 49) became seriously interested in photography shortly after high school when her mother lent her a 35mm rangefinder. She says, "I took photos every chance I had, and it seems the more difficult the opportunity, the more I enjoy it. From sunrise to sunset I see everything as though looking through a viewfinder. My strong interest has led me into the darkroom, where I enjoy spending a lot of time."

Jim Sokolik (pp. 106–7, 112) began his involvement with photography with a desire to document the life and culture of distant lands. Later, he became aware of the visual richness of St. Louis, his hometown. He spends many hours exploring the city and photographing its people and architecture. Doing his own darkroom work has been an important and creative part of his photography. His work has been exhibited and published in the St. Louis area.

127

Christine Struttman (p. 55), who lives in rural central Missouri, has a full-time job and takes pictures only as a hobby now, but would eventually like to pursue it as a full-time career. No particular subject is her favorite; she enjoys all outdoor photography. Recently she has become more involved in macro photography and finds it interesting. She is a member of the National Wildlife Federation and supports the preservation of America.

Mark A. Styles (p. 63) is a lifelong resident of Kansas City, Missouri. He says that he "only recently resumed his photographic interest after he had secured his family's lifestyle." Mark's photographic background includes experience at the Kansas City Art Institute and Penn Valley College, and he is a member of the Photographic Society of America. He now works for an area news publication. He has a knack for capturing the mood of his subjects.

Nancy L. Thompson (p. 68), a rural Missouri native and a photography graduate of Northeast Missouri State University, has been photographing landscapes and country scenes for a number of years. Working primarily in color, she has chosen as her main subject the clear-water streams of the Ozarks and the old mills that accompany many of them. She hopes that through her photography, she can help to preserve the natural beauty of Missouri for future generations.

Thomas Trodgon (pp. 22, 89, 95) has been capturing the Missouri landscape for more than ten years. His publication credits include books, magazines, calendars, and greeting cards. Missouri is a playground of unique moments for a photographer, Thomas believes, because of the diverse nature of the state. Thomas recently received his M.B.A. from the University of Missouri–Columbia.

Blaine A. Ulmer (p. 62) has spent his adult life in Missouri and has hunted and fished throughout the state. Since retiring from his own sales engineering business, he has become active in state and national environmental and conservation organizations. His major hobby, however, is nature photography in the field and in the darkroom.

David Ulmer (pp. 1, 71, 82–83), when not doing commercial assignments, pursues the quixotic quest of nature photographers in search of the holy grail, an *Audubon* cover shot. Short of that, his work has appeared in *Natural History, Sierra,* and *Missouri Conservationist.* He is the son of Blaine Ulmer, also represented in this book.

Curtis N. VanWye (p. 18) has been involved in photography since the age of ten, when his father gave him his first 35mm camera. Currently employed by Columbia Photo & Video, he has had experience in nearly every aspect of photography. But his true love is his personal work, which has received awards at various outdoor art fairs throughout the state over the past ten years. Recently he has been concentrating on being published and pursuing gallery showings.

Rickard Walk (pp. 14, 34, 76, 77), a certified registered nurse anesthetist, has pursued his interest in photography more intensely since becoming a member of the Mid-Missouri Camera Club and the Chouteau Grotto Cave and Outdoor Club. He is an active climber, backpacker, and caver. He has combined his enthusiasm for the outdoors with photography to provide educational lap-and-dissolve shows for community groups and schools.

David J. Walker (pp. 45, 52) became interested in photography in 1965 during his tour of duty in Vietnam. His main interest is in the composition and presentation of the art.

Tony Weil (pp. 21, 90) has only pursued photography for a year. Now serving in the Air Force, he is considering a career in photography. He shot the photographs published in this book on his family's farm in Columbia with his new Maxxum 7000. He studied photography under the critical eye of a photographer friend. Tony says that he is "only twenty years old and still learning."

Charles Weishaupt (p. 121), a media specialist and teacher at Carlinville (Illinois) High School, has practiced photography both as a hobby and as a way of helping his school's yearbook. Using both black and white and color, he works primarily with a view camera; his large- and medium-format transparencies are sold through Photographic Resources, a St. Louis stock agency.

Gregory Wolff (pp. 19, 31) is an art student specializing in graphic design. His love for photography has inspired him to study it as both a fine and graphic art. Although his primary interest is photojournalism, that pursuit has given him many opportunities to photograph Missouri's environment. He plans a career that combines photography with the graphic arts.

Library of Congress Cataloging-in-Publication Data
Colorful Missouri.
    1. Missouri—Description and travel—
1981-   —Views. I. King, Edward. II. Nunn, Bill.
F467.C66 1988   977.8'0022'2   88-4781
ISBN 0-8262-0680-8 (alk. paper)